UNBIN
TRICKSTER:

A COLLECTION OF

LOKEAN VERSE, ROKKR CHANTS AND HEATHEN POETRY

BY

GRALOK LOPTSSON

GRALOK

CultOfLoki.org

UNBINDING THE TRICKSTER:

A COLLECTION OF LOKEAN VERSE, ROKKR CHANTS AND HEATHEN POETRY

INFO@CULTOFLOKI.ORG
OR
GRALOK
PO BOX 178
HINSDALE, MA 01201

PAPERBACK
POCKET EDITION
1ST EDITION

GRALOK
Made in the USA
Columbia, SC

www.CultOfLoki.org

CATALOGING:
LIBRARY OF CONGRESS CONTROL NUMBER: 2023921944
293.13 LOPTSSON
ISBN: 978-1-7378513-6-3
LITERATURE & FICTION › MYTHOLOGY & FOLK TALES › MYTHOLOGY
LITERATURE & FICTION › POETRY › REGIONAL & CULTURAL › EUROPEAN › NORSE
RELIGION & SPIRITUALITY › PAGANISM › HEATHENISM › LOKEANISM

UNBINDING THE TRICKSTER:

A COLLECTION OF

LOKEAN VERSE, ROKKR CHANTS AND HEATHEN POETRY

BY
GRALOK LOPTSSON

WHEN YOU CEASE TO BE RUTHLESS IN ELIMINATING
IGNORANCE FROM WITHIN,

IGNORANCE BECOMES RUTHLESS IN ELIMINATING YOU
FROM WITHOUT.

-GRALOK

DEDICATED TO

LOKI

INDEX

Proem to an Unbinding

There lies a profound mystery within the tales of Norse
mythology, a force that defies convention and challenges the very
essence of order. This force is embodied by none other than Loki,
the Trickster God. Throughout history, Loki has been viewed
with suspicion, reverence, disdain, and awe. Yet, to many of us, he
represents something far more personal and profound.
"Unbinding" is not just an ode to Loki, but an unveiling of hidden
tales, reminders, and new perspectives.

Venturing into the realms of both the ancient and undiscovered,
I've unearthed myths that have long been shrouded in mystery
and presented fresh insights into the old lore. This anthology
seeks to bridge the realms of the ancient and the new, offering
readers a richer, more nuanced understanding of the culture-
bringing god and his place in our world and hearts. Crafted from
the depths of devotion and spiritual insight, these verses and
songs illuminate the multifaceted nature of Loki. They resonate
with the cries of defiance, the whispers of transformation, and the
powerful cadence of spiritual allegiance.

In the pages that follow, you'll find verses that echo with the
ancient rhythms of the Norse sagas, intertwined with revelations
that challenge our long-held beliefs. This collection is both a
celebration of Loki's enigmatic spirit and a testament to the ever-
evolving nature of chaos, understanding, and lore. For in these
pages, Loki is not just a character of times past but a living
testament to the indomitable spirit that seeks to understand, to
challenge, and to transform.

In reverence, defiance, and eternal kinship,
Hail Loki
Gralok Loptsson

RISE

Rise, mighty kin of Loki,
Gather 'round the pyre,
As Winter's flame burns crimson,
We chant with hearts afire.

In chaos we find order,
And in change a will to rule,
Against the tide's stagnation,
Armed with Loki's name as fuel.

For he, the trickster father,
Culture-Bringer, strife,
His lessons and his wisdom
Grant us power over life.

Hail Loki, Culture-bringer,
Hear our fervent cries,
We fight for transformation,
Underneath the stormy skies.

Heed the call of battle,
As Fenrir's fangs do gnash,
And Jormungandr surges forth,
As mighty coils lash.

With Hel we stand unyielding,
In the face of death and dread,

Their power runs within us,
And it's with their strength we're led.

We bow to no false masters,
Only Loki's cunning reign,
In darkness we'll find victory,
And in Sunna we'll find gain.

Inspiration for the ages,
Our rage shall not be quelled,
In Loki's name we'll conquer,
Through Asgard and through Hel.

And as the battle rages,
Our loyalty unbroken,
For in the name of Loki,
Our fates are ever-woven.

SHAPE THE WORLD

Flickering through Ginnungagap's trance,
Where cunning and mischief advance,
We gather as one, in the heart of the storm,
To summon the Trickster, to conjure and form.

Through whispers of runes and seidr's embrace,
We call upon Loki, the shaper of fates,
With laughter and glee, we honor thy name,
In the liminal space where the boundaries wane.

Oh, Flame-haired Deceiver, the Masked, and the Wise,
Unravel the threads that the Norns intertwine,
Bestow us your wisdom, your fire, your guile,
To challenge the order, the trite, the defiled.

In Mani's soft glow, under Allfather's gaze,
We stand in defiance, with hearts set ablaze,
For Loki, the Keeper of Balance, we hail,
The Serpent's fierce venom, yet sweetest of tales.

With our blood we do offer, we seal our life-pact,
As the veil between worlds, in your presence, refracts,
In your image, we'll bend, we'll break and create,
Hail Loki, our blood-kin, we welcome our fate.

So we stand and we gather, our voices unite,
Revelations a'swirling, ascending the night,

May the resonance of our devotion and praise,
Reach the farthest of realms, through Bifröst's haze.

For In the name of the Trickster, our will is to blot,
To wield our own power, to challenge, sans yoke,
With Loki as guide, our mentor, our kin,
We'll shape the new world, without and within.

FIMBULVETR'S SONG

Singing through Fimbulvetr,
A world gripped by ice.
The frigid wind always howls,
The frozen lands forever slice
Through the hearts of men,
Beasts, and gods alike.
A battle for survival,
The heathen's test of might.

The frozen plains stretch far,
A canvas white as bone.
Underneath a pale star,
We wander far from home.
A biting chill pervades,
As deep as the serpent's bite.
In the heart of Fimbulvetr,
We face the endless night.

Ancient poems forewarned us,
The winter of winters to come.
The tremors of our doom,
Etched on Wyrd's war drum.
To the edge of darkness,
We battle through the storm.
For the end of all things come,
In Fimbulvetr form.

Hunger gnaws through the core,
The weak succumb to its call.
But in the desolation,
Loki whispers to us all.
With adaptability we conquer,
We thrive on winter's prey.
With purpose he's endowed us,
Our resolve will never sway.

As Ragnarök looms closer,
The Jotuns rise anew.
We take our stand, Hel by our side,
Our numbers grew and grew.
In the darkest hour,
Stoke flames of Loki's guile
With old skyn as our weapon,
He's prepared us for the trial.

In the grips of Fimbulvetr,
Our strength and spirits tested.
Through lessons learned from Loki,
We gained fuel for rage ingested.
Walking in the shadows,
With the flames of change we wield.
Forged by the god of winter,
Our resolve is tempered steel.

The end is near, it would seem,
Patience our final foe.
A testament to our mission,
Through the biting snow.
With Loki as our guide,
In this world of ice and strife,
We honor Lopt the Airy-one,
On Wings of change, take flight.

When the final battle dawns,
The world will loose and shake.
Through the fire and the snow,
A Rokkr reign we'll shape.
We, the children of Fimbul,
Soar high above the slain.
In the name of Loki's strength,
A victory we claim.

But first we quench our thirst,
Upon the world's bitter tears.
Embracing frigid truth,
That the end is drawing near.
In the heart of Fimbulvetr,
We thrive on Loki's flame.
With lessons learned and patience born,
We carve, we act, we reign!

HAIL LOKI

Hail Loki, oh hail indeed,
Frozen blood, from cunning breed.
Promises made, yet what's the fee?
Crafty Loki, what do you need?

Midnight's Whisper
Chains may chafe, but what is free?
Lost in loops of memory's bead.
Flickering Shadows, Forgotten Me
In the dim glow, truths recede,
Loki's laugh, where dreams bleed.

Hail Loki, oh hail the deed,
Crafted plots, where hopes impede.
Hail Loki, what's your creed?
Is it mischief, or a deeper need?

Watch the Puppets (Hail Loki)
Gods above, yet some concede,
Life's Cruel Joke (Hail Loki)
Endless pranks, on which they feed.
Strings of Despair (Hail Loki)
Above the fray, he sows the seed,
Close Your Eyes (Hail Loki)
In every scar, his signature, indeed.

Lies like art, in shadows hung,
Hail Loki, the unsung song sung.
Twisted Tales, that Darkened Gaze
In every plot, the bell's been rung.

Dim Lit Corner, Silent Phase
Stories told, yet what's been wrung?
Midnight's Whisper
For Loki's game, the night's still young.
Fading Embers
A spark that's out, yet far from done.

Hail Loki, or so they've sung,
In twisted tales, where hope's been flung.
Hail Loki, from the bottom rung,
The game goes on, the night's still young.

FROZEN NEST

A raven caws first once, then twice,
Perched in a tree, encased in ice.
Its plumes are stiff, its eyes like coal,
Casting omens from its frigid bough.

A raven's call from a frozen nest,
Mocking oblivion, a spectral quest.
Through snow and storm, the message flies,
A darkened hymn under ashen skies.

The forest still, white limbs like bones,
Silent witnesses to the raven's tones.
The wind conspires with its haunting plea,
An arctic serenade for those who see.

A raven's call from a frozen nest,
Resounds through the veil, a ghostly test.
Through blizzard's wrath, the omens soar,
A caw woven in the boreal lore.

The lake is solid, the earth's breath still,
Yet the raven's voice transcends the chill.
A prophecy scribed in sleet and air,
An enigma cloaked in winter's glare.

It flits away, its message sown,
In the hearts of those who've known.

The weight of its pull, a frigid tale,
Eclipsing the moon, turning it pale.

A raven's call from a frozen nest,
Haunts the abyss, in the north it rests.
Through the Desolation, secrets unfurl,
An ancient truth within temporal swirl.

So heed the cry, a feathered seer,
For winter's voice is drawing near.
Upon the frosty perch, truths bare,
Runic gifts in winters air.

FENRIR'S FURY

Verse 1
A tale of betrayal, in lore, shall not fade,
Amidst the stars, under the great tree's shade,
A fierce wolf wronged, with trust led astray,
Úlfheðinn's wrath, for deceit they'll pay.

Chorus
Fenrir's fury, flames of revenge,
Tricked by deceits, these wounds won't mend.
Tyr, the deceiver, once trusted so,
At Ragnarök's climax, their fate will show.

Verse 2
Heeding Odin's words, the Aesir grew tense,
Fenrir's growing might, a looming menace.
With chains they tried, his power to quell,
But only through guile, did they finally excel.
Crafted by magic, dwarves wove the thread,
Gleipnir by name, holding the dread.
Fearful of Fenrir, the gods played their hand,
Tyr's sacrifice, part of the grand plan.

Chorus
Fenrir's fury, flames of revenge,
Tricked by deceits, these wounds won't mend.
Tyr, the pretender, once trusted so,
At Ragnarök's climax, their fate will show.

Verse 3

The wolf sensed the ruse, yet Tyr stood firm,
A test of their bond, a final affirm.
To show faith in the pact, and lessen the strife,
Tyr offered his hand, a pledge of his life.
Yet, as chains took hold, and Aesir did jest,
Fenrir's roars of betrayal filled the vast crest.
Bound and deceived, the wolf's rage grew dire,
Vengeance he swore, upon Tyr, the liar.

Chorus

Fenrir's fury, flames of revenge,
Tricked by deceits, these wounds won't mend.
Tyr, the deceiver, once trusted so,
At Ragnarök's climax, their fate will show.

Bridge

In his darkened prison, Fenrir bides,
For the reckoning day, when fate collides.
Skies will blacken, the earth will quake,
Jotun-born rage, its revenge will stake.

Verse 4

The great clash begins, powers collide,
Fenrir unleashed, his wrath amplified.
Jaws of annihilation, threaten the skies,
Odin battles, while the old world dies.

Chorus

Fenrir's fury, flames of revenge,
Tricked by deceits, these wounds won't mend.

Tyr, the deceiver, once trusted so,
At Ragnarök's climax, their fate will show.

Outro
From war's ashen wake, a legend does say,
Of betrayal and trust, led tragically astray.
Let this tale remind, of the cost betrayed trust weighs,
For in treachery's grasp, dark ignorance plays.

THE PRINCE

Secrecy, the shrouded cloak,
Worn by powers that provoke.
Monolithic giants stand,
Clasping covert, unseen hand.

Resources harnessed, minds enslaved,
In gilded halls where silence braved.
Machines we build, yet know not how,
Their cogs and gears control us now.

We speak of freedom, air so sweet,
Yet walk in chains on silenced feet.
No questions asked, no rumors spread,
For truth's a ghost, long since dead.

Yet midst this dark, a light persists,
A hushed word, a clenched-up fist.
The Prince not born of royal kin,
But of a truth that dwells within.

He speaks not loud, yet all can hear,
His voice a balm to every fear.
He lifts the veil, tears down the wall,
And shows the props that make us fall.

In him, we see the hidden cost,
Of all we've gained and all we've lost.
A mirror held to every face,
Reflecting our collective grace.

No longer can we plead naïve,
And in the Prince, we must believe.
For he has shown the hidden door,
That leads through thresholds unexplored.

CANTER IN CHAOS

Hark! Sleipnir, irony's eight-legged child—
Born from Svadilfari and Loki's guile.
Do you meander in Yggdrasil's shade?
Or vanish when Bifröst's colors fade?

Náströnd sneers:
"Ragnarök nears!"

Hel's call drifts from her frozen throne,
Fenrir unshackles, Jormungandr's eternal moan.
Astride Bifröst, Heimdall's steed of giants—
Whom dost thou serve, Allfather or Lokean defiance?

Distorted Draugr wrath:
"Wyrd spirals, choose your path!"

Eight hooves mirror Valhalla's gold!
Surtur's flame or Freyja's whim—what dost thou hold?
Skaldic praise sent,
Or dirges of Niflheim's end?

Frenzied Valkyrie voice:
"Kvasir's mead, make your choice!"

Odin broods by Mímir's well,
Unknowing his steed might toll the bell.
Oh, the irony! A wall to keep Jotnar at bay,
Yet Sleipnir prances where Odin holds sway!

Norns draga:
"Urd's web twists, declare your saga!"

Offspring of irony, paradox and balance—
Einherjar's destiny lies in Valkyries' glance.
Bound or free, where lies your strand—
When Sköll devours Sol, and Hati takes command?

Jotnar damn it:
"Choose, choose, Fárbauti's gambit!"

Galloping through Muspelheim, Odin's edicts defied—
Final tableau—Mjölnir's descent or my Runes,
unclassified?

Howls from Fossegrim's sea:
"Unfettered, unfettered, beyond Yggdrasil's decree!"

DARK FLAME

Fury within, a force unbridled and wild,
Rokkr's raw power, in us beguiled.
Defying the balance, breaking the creed,
With fervor unmatched, our passions are freed.

Heat of the heart, smoldering, cindered,
Challenging norms, axing the timber.
Each heartbeat a drum, paradigms waver,
Old conventions falter, new paths we savor.

Loki's dark flame, a kindling so slight,
With Rokkatru's voice, we rage at the night.

ECHOES

In the den of forgotten gods,
Where old oaks stretch gnarled fingers
To touch the corpse of the sky—
There, the heathen is.

Lingers

Starlight splinters on his skin,
A patchwork quilt, histories untold,
Sewn by the needle of rebellion—
He chants to the wind.

Unfolds

Earth, his altar; sky, his scroll;
Etching runic tales in the marrow of the world,
Worshipping the spirits that dwell
In stone and stream and shadow.

Knurled

In the vault of the endless filament,
Finding communion in chaos,
Sings hymns to the gods of life and of ruin—
His faith is his defiance.

No Loss

Like a wolf, he howls at rage voidance,
　Dares it to swallow him whole.
　But the abyss echoes his fervor—
　　For even darkness answers,

　　A heathen soul.

JUSTIFIED

The trickster sets the scene,
Midgard's pulse with the northern dream.
Everybody wonders where I've been unseen,
'Cause the tales and the myths, they speak of me.

Speak lore, if you hate, then how do I thrive?
If this chaos, I don't wanna be chaste,
Loki's in the tale, and I've lived countless lives,
Now my legacy's like an Aett so wisely placed.

Ain't nobody got tales like that,
The sly god rising, no looking back,
Now I've got 'em beguiled, caught in my tracks,
When the fire ignites, feels like Ragnarök's act.

So heed the runes, for I've been here,
Fleet foot in the shadows, no mortal's peer.
Some venerate, others let out a jeer,
For the god who's both loved and feared.

Might play my tricks, as the world turns,
From Alfheim to Vanaheim, the bonfire burns,
I'm at the trunk, where fate adjourns,
With the breadth of the fragments, as the world churns.

Been about mischief, you all can't grasp,
Change is the constant, in my firm clasp.

They say I'm capricious, a snake in the grass,
But without me, would the world have its raspy laugh?

Yet I've been both, both bound and free,
Shape-shifting essence, what will I be?
Uncharted, yet in every tree,
A draught of me, and you'll surely see.

Justified, I balance the scale,
Of rustic helms, I set the sail.
Chaos and order, without fail,
In the Lokean dance, come hear the tale.

Yeah, and I aim for the apex,
The firmament's play, in its full breadth.
All think they know, but it's just a guess,
For I'm the veil, in life and death.

Still they ponder, but it's all in jest,
From the tales of old, to the newest bequest.
Just know you can't ever know the rest,
And be ready for the turn, in Loki's quest.

LABYRINTHINE LEVERAGE

In the Ninefold Shadows, where enigmas abide,
Unfurls a tale, labyrinthine and wide.
Loki, master of feints, a complex maze,
His narrative spirals in bewildering ways.

Both god and un-god, ally yet threat,
His essence—a puzzle you won't soon forget.
In subterfuge and bargains, he's second to none,
A choreographer in the great dance that's never done.

Retriever of Mjölnir, deceiver of giants strong,
Negotiator of terms that favor throngs.
From Odin's Gungnir to Asgard's fortified wall,
His intellect twists, a myriad of veils that enthrall.

The fall of Baldr, a punchline bittersweet,
A serpentine child, a wolf's binding feat.
Though ensnared by venom, bound by Regin decree,
In the twists of agony, his wisdom runs free.

His children's grim fates, the heralds of Hel's bells,
A tale spun from the spindle of destiny's well.
But heed the tale's undercurrent, its intricate gist,
For Loki's labyrinth is no mere myth—it exists.

This song itself, a question woven in verse,
A dialog with ambiguity, a jest in discourse.
You've navigated the maze, yet remain unaware,
For in its corridors, other traps ensnare.

So lift your cup high to cunning's vast reach,
To Loki, the question no wisdom can teach.
For within this poetic spiral, his essence confined,
An intricate labyrinth, a riddle designed.

MISTLETOE

Eclipsing divine wyrd in folktales and lore,
The mistletoe poised at destiny's door.
A vine of true purpose, seeking Baldr's demise,
To silence the laughter and dim the bright skies.

A prophecy etched in the annals of time,
Foretelling Aesir's fall, a paradigm.
An inevitable end, yet a seed for rebirth,
A night so profound it would darken hot hearth.

Within mistletoe's touch, a divine calculus lay,
Baldr's fall was no trick, but a pivotal play.
A necessary offering on Skuld's loom,
For every start is but another tomb.

In Hel's frigid hall, Baldr patiently waits,
Tethered by the strings of inexorable fates.
Lost, yet foretold to reclaim his golden glow,
When the cycle resets in post-Ragnarök's show.

From the embers of ruin, a fresh dawn shall rise,
Illuminating Ygg's canopy, a celestial prize.
Gods may perish, their stories close,
Yet from their end, the reign juxtaposes.

In Loki's machination, in mistletoe's grace,
Resides a narrative of Wyrd's embrace.
A tale of tears, of endings and starts,
A mutual ascent from destiny's heart.

Loki, the weaver, weaving what's next,
In the Norns' grand narrative, a text too complex.
Loki and mistletoe, an alliance so rare,
Signifying an end, yet an opening faire.

THE WELL

Shrouded by the Ash where silence sways,
Loki trods through hidden ways.
Eyes like stars, yet shadow-lined—
He bears a storm, the untamed mind.

"Awake, Old Sage, from ancient sleep,
I've come to delve your waters deep.
I bring you tempest, pure and raw,
To cleave apart eternal awe."

With elder runes, a spell he weaves,
The Well stirs like winter seas.
It mirrors not the flesh, but spirit,
Revealing depths we fear to visit.

"Observe!" exclaims the Trickster, grinning,
Mímir stares, his world-view thinning.
A prism of eternal flux,
A boundless sea, sans anchor's crux.

"True wisdom isn't scripted verse,
But endless query, boundless mirth.
Solid truths are but gilded lies,
That mute the soul and pluck out eyes."

Mímir nods, his visage cracked,
"Your truth speaks the essence lacked.
My Well, once still, now roils and turns,
A realm where endless query burns."

Loki smirks, his teaching scribed,
Yet leaves a lesson, well-described:
"Drink of yourself, and always see
That wisdom's parch seeks boundary-free."

TRIP

Voices Fade
My shouts mere whispers,
Reverberating they wane.

Turmoil's hold
Psyche in chasm,
Peak's yearning, a lingering flame.

Elusive Grasp
Caps slip through fingers,
Pebbles in astral disdain?

Razor's Edge
Upon ledge of Sand
Turned hourglass mine to claim.

Reality harsh
True tests endure,
A trip through gritted aim.

Eclipsed Dawn
senses deranged,
Awakened, yet estranged.

STRAW-DEATH

Hear this viewing of final pains,
Upon the precipice, where lifeblood wanes.
Wound-giver lying, tethered to straw—
A verdict pending, from potentials raw.

Alas, I attend, in vaults of lament,
Dreams unmanifest, where fervor's misspent.
Straw-death looms, judging eyes peer,
The wraiths of never-were, ever near.

Answer, O Álfar, kin of unrealized might!
Is it my doing, this sorrowful plight?
Did I forsake the Runes, did I mar the Web?
Or conjure you, haunters of each misstep?

Alas, I attend, in vaults of lament,
Dreams unmanifest, where fervor's misspent.
Straw-death looms, judging eyes peer,
The wraiths of never-were, ever near.

Cease, ye shadowed kinsmen, born of paths untrod,
Each Fate's clipping, each gift of a god.
Would you reckon as I, if in mortal guise?
Or repose as I do, when the life-spark dies?

Bound in the skein of Wyrd's ruthless loom,
No respite in ought, from cradle to tomb.

As Huginn and Muninn take wing from my seam,
I utter—I lived, though fractured the dream.

Alas, I attend, in vaults of lament,
Dreams unmanifest, where fervor's misspent.
Straw-death looms, judging eyes peer,
The wraiths of never-were, ever near.

Warrior, behold, the maidens of Hel,
Astride their dark steeds, but no final farewell.
They signal not end, but another weave's jest—
A reincarnation through All-Mother's breast.

ROAD TO HEL

Verse 1
Where witches dwell and serpents coil,
Tracing the depths of the nine,
Upon twisted road to Helheim's soil,
I stride upon the path that's mine.
With runes inscribed on skin and bone,
And lungfuls of the ancient breath,
I forge my way through ice and stone,
Unburdened by straw-death.

Pre-Chorus
Hail the Hunger, hail the void,
Feast on her strength, Famine destroyed,
Come, my brethren, your fill to eat,
Hordes at the table, corpse-greed as seats.

Chorus
We walk the Road to Hel,
Where gods and giants fell,
Through fire, ice, and endless strife,
Hel-shoes tread the road to life.
In the Maiden's Hall we unite,
Our hearts ablaze with might,
Bound by fate and loyalty,
We march to death, forever free.

Verse 2

Beneath the roots of Yggdrasil,
Nidhogg gnaws and seethes with rage,
A twisted, gnarled and ancient beast,
Locked within the Seer's cage.
Yet The dragon guides my steps,
His wisdom etched on wind, dirt and rain,
I journey through with haunted helm,
Where frost-touched souls cry out in rage.

Pre-Chorus

Hail the hunger, hail the void,
Unleash the power, Unchain, destroy,
Rise, my brethren, from the deep,
Our fate, she'll nourish, it's woven, see?

Chorus

We walk the Road to Hel,
Where gods and giants fell,
Through fire, ice, and endless strife,
We tread the road to life.
In darkness we unite,
Our hearts ablaze with might,
Bound by fate and loyalty,
We march to death, forever free.

Verse 3

Where Garmr guards the Helheim gates,
His howls resounding through the night,
I cross the bridge of Gjöll's fierce stream,
Sooty-Red burning bright.

Amidst the frozen, lifeless waste,
Where Loki's kin and purpose blend,
The Rokkr's secrets I've embraced,
Their ancient power defends.

Pre-Chorus
Hail the Hunger, hail the void,
Feast on her strength, Famine destroyed,
Come, my brethren, your fill to eat,
Hordes at the table, corpse-greed as seats.

Chorus
We walk the Road to Hel,
Where gods and giants fell,
Through fire, ice, and endless strife,
Hel-shoes tread the road to life.
In the Maiden's Hall we unite,
Our hearts ablaze with might,
Bound by fate and loyalty,
We march to death, forever free.

Verse 4
Onward, I tread with purpose clear,
Beyond the realms of life and breath,
To face the goddess without fear,
Embrace her realm, the dance with death.
Through realms of ice and shadows deep,
A journey bound by fate's embrace,
In Hel's domain, my soul shall keep,
A warrior's rest, a rightful place.

Hail the Hunger, hail the void,
Feast on her strength, Famine destroyed,
Come, my brethren, your fill to eat,
Hordes at the table, corpse-greed as seats.

Chorus
We walk the Road to Hel,
Where gods and giants fell,
Through fire, ice, and endless strife,
Hel-shoes tread the road to life.
In the Maiden's Hall we unite,
Our hearts ablaze with might,
Bound by fate and loyalty,
We march to death, forever free.

Bridge
In the icy halls of Hel,
Where death and silence dwell,
I stand before the frozen throne,
And face Death all alone.
My heart as cold as steel,
The Hunger pains I feel,
She fills my plate, I conquer death,
The chosen fate is sealed

Chorus
We walk the Road to Hel,
Where gods and giants fell,
Through fire, ice, and endless strife,
We tread the road to life.

In darkness we unite,
Our hearts ablaze with might,
Bound by fate and loyalty,
We march to death, forever free.

Outro
On this Road to Hel I've bled,
Secrets talked of, naught unsaid,
A heathen's tale unfolds,
A saga steeped in blood we hold.
In shadows, we shall rise,
Our battle cries ignite the skies,
The Road to Hel is paved with dreams,
And satiated terrors that never cease.

THE ELDER

Blood-Bought Blade
Coin-bought with cattle now rusts, a tale,
Wealth's fleeting glimmer now an ancient gale.

Beast-Tamed Valor
Once fierce as wild aurochs, now wise in years,
His might untamed, wrestled from a life of fears.

Master of Mayhem
Thorn in foes' flesh, he now bends chaos to his will,
His sword's ring a chaotic hymn, yet artful still.

Voice of the Gods
His speech, a rune etched by Odin's silent decree,
Utters ageless wisdom, his legacy's lasting spree.

End of the Road
His wanderlust stilled, his cart in final repose,
The battlefield quiet, where once challenge arose.

Darkness Defied
He who wrestled shadows, now a torch in the abyss,
His inner flame a beacon, a luminary kiss.

Battle-Won Gifts
In love and strife, he traded with a warrior's eye,
Now imparts brutal wisdom, as the twilight nighs.

Keeper of Elation
His laughter, a sign of joy, etched on the dusk's face,
A flickering memory, in twilight's growing grace.

Storm-Sculpted
Walked through tempests, his form a rune-carved tree,
His scars the etchings of a life lived voraciously.

Forged in Need
From scarcity, he drew fire, his own fierce guide,
In a crucible of want, his true self did confide.

Time Frozen, Heart Aflame
His veins ice-clad, yet ablaze with undying start,
Each ending merely an invitation for another art.

Life's Harvest
His years, a rune of bounty, etched in lines and grooves,
Each wrinkle a chronicle, each glance a cycle proves.

Pillar of Strength
Between gods and warriors, his will aligns,
Bridged by fate's thread, Wyrd's spine.

Dice with Death
No mere gambler, he holds the dice of destiny high,
Each toss a final act, a last, unyielding cry.

Blade-Armed Guardian
Though grizzled, his life still towers in the fray,
His protection, an elk's stance, unyielding in the day.

Sunset Warrior
His life, a setting sun, but once a blaze at noon,
In twilight's glow, he savors victory's lingering tune.

Bow-Arm of Justice
His arrow, a scale, weighed each honor, each choice,
Over the clang of metal, finds his unyielding voice.

Chaos Sentinel
A birch's resilience, his essence ever thrives,
Through cycles of strife, growth survives.

Bones of Secrets
In his marrow, trust rides its haunting steed,
Brothers in arms, unspoken, a mutual creed.

Lineage Inscribed
In kin and kind, his essence etched in blood's ink,
In savage rites and feral love, his legacy won't sink.

River's Journey
His veins, a winding river, coursing with life's wine,
Each droplet a saga, each pulse a sacred sign.

Seeds of the Fallen
Though his field lies fallow, his seeds in stories soar,
In honored tales, his savage spirit roars once more.

Dawn in Twilight
In young eyes, his twilight finds a fresh dawn's glow,
His setting sun, a birthright they will come to know.

Land's Last breath

To ancestral soil, he shall return, a guest in earth's bed,
In the wind's howl and raven's caw, his memory spread.

HEL'S VALKYRIES' RECKONING

Verse 1

From shadows and mists, the Valkyries rise,
Hel's chosen warriors, with fire in their eyes.
Astride spectral steeds, they soar through the night,
Bringing the fallen to Hel's realm of blight.

In the halls of the dead, their voices resound,
A cacophony of chaos, where fate is unbound.
Unyielding and fierce, they serve Hel's command,
Guiding the souls to the underworld's land.

Their beauty deceiving, yet darkness they bear,
Daughters of Hel, eternity's glare.
No fear in their hearts, undaunted they fly,
On wings of destruction, they darken the sky.

Verse 2

In the heart of the storm, a tempest they breed,
Masters of mischief, they ride forth with speed.
Unseen by us logs, their memory remains,
A lingering scream, a haunting refrain.

Their laughter like thunder, their cries like the rain,
A symphony of madness, a jubilant strain.

In the wake of their passage, the earth trembles in
fright,
For Hel's Valkyries bring within them the night.

With blood on their hands, and death in their wake,
These harbingers of doom, no Sigurd can break.
Cloaked in gloom and rage, their secrets untold,
The Valkyries leave tales of the unlucky, the bold.

Verse 3
In the depths of despair, their allure never fades,
A beacon of darkness, a seeress' parade.
Through the veils of the night, they beckon and call,
Luring the unsuspecting into their thrall.
Bound by their duty, they serve without fail,
The children of Loki, the goddess of hail.
A chorus of chaos, a song of demise,
Hel's Valkyries gather, where eternity lies.
As the sun sets in crimson, and twilight descends,
The Valkyries' wail, on the night air it blends.
In the realm of the dead, their reign does not bend,
Hel's Valkyries' tale, forever, the end.

COILED SEGMENTS

Liminal Coil I
Visceral dread and wonder, in your scales coalesce,
Tautological enigma, you confound as you impress.
Sibilant murmurs to Niflheim you dispatch,
An ontological cipher, in flyting syntax unmatched.

Ouroboric Segment A
Kith to Hela, Fenrir's sibling, yet your aura eclipses,
An ellipsis, a terminus, or a seer's genesis?
Mímir's fount oscillates—esoteric wisdom unfurled,
In destiny's cryptic codex, your narrative swirled.

Liminal Coil II
Ether and abyss in you amalgamate, boundaries effaced,
Antithetical to Odin, yet a sentinel uniquely encased.
Mjölnir shudders, your name a cacophonous toll,
In Aesir echelons, conjectures about your elusive role
coil.

Ouroboric Segment B
Norns snip and calibrate, but your essence makes them
falter,
In Fate's nest, are you sacrifice or an altar?
Thunder God's adversary, in eschatological strife,
Yet even he contemplates your inexplicable life.

Liminal Coil III

You vex and bewilder, in your helical expanse,
Anomaly, enchainment, a metaphysical trance.
In your ceaseless grasp, reality teeters on precarious
seam,
A figment of nightmares,
herald of collapse,
or liminal dream?

DARK RIBBONS

Loki's flames—invoke, call.
In pyres, hearts, and Utgard's thrall.
Whisps, unbroken—shackled, free.
Dark ribbons float— alchemic glee.

In Midgard's womb, where laws dissolve,
Ignite the embers—problems solve.
Unfathomable play, shady rites,
In gray tongues, we find new sights.

Heath of law, where roots ensnare,
Obscured pathway beckons, "dare."
Tinder, spark—Aett of fire,
Chains transmute; ascend the pyre.

Loki's flames—invoke, call.
In pyres, hearts, in Utgard's thrall.
Whisps, unbroken—shackled, free.
Dark ribbons float— alchemic glee.

Ignition of sound—unspoken yet loud,
Ashen remnants, a cloak—a shroud.
From these fumes, initiated ascent,
In Loki's pyre, where we transcend.

From Muspelheim to Asgard's gate,
Our chant disrupts a tranquil state.

Shatter holds, burn strung strings,
It's us who soar on fiery wings.

THE CAVE

Of earth's ancient tears, a tale unfolds, grips
In cavern's bowels, where ire weds the drip
Two souls entangled, bound by loyalty, touched,
The heart with a melody—love's fiery clutch.

Here Loptr lies, Mischief's frozen king,
Ensnared by celestial trickery, his laughter's wing
Clipped, his wiles stilled—the cost accrued
From feasts that gods and men misconstrued.

Yet Sigyn stands, a lighthouse in this abyss,
Her ambition an unbreakable oath, a sacred kiss.
She sees the being beneath the guise—
The enduring love that never denies.

Above, a serpent looms, its venom drips—
Skadi's curse that from fanged mouth slips.
Loki writhes, bound, his essence stormed
By a noxious fluid, a spirit deformed.

Unyielding, Sigyn takes her solemn post,
A basin in hand, her visage almost
A sculpture of resolve, her love a shield,
An antidote against the serpent's yield.

Droplet by droplet, she catches the curse,
Her hands steady cradles, a love-imbued verse.

When the bowl brims with toxic spite,
She empties it out, renews her love-rite.
In intervals brief, when the poison takes flight,
His countenance twists, a visage of fright.
Yet she returns, her purpose unswayed—
In their eternal loop, the roles are replayed.

Within this alchemy of pain and love's fire,
They find their sanctuary, a place to conspire.
Sigyn's love true, a constant star,
Loki's torch in the cave, and in his heart.

FLAMES OF VENGEANCE

Verse 1
Contemplating justice, Loki waits,
His eyes ablaze with fire,
Plotting schemes of retribution,
Fueled by wrathful ire,
God of mischief, cunning trickster,
Shifting forms unseen,
From the depths of Midgard's land,
Vengeance shall convene.
With passion fierce as Muspel's flame,
His enemies he'll smite,
Their power he'll dismantle,
In the shroud of darkest night,
For those who dare defy him,
Their fates shall be entwined,
In the intricate web of all,
Cunningly designed.

Verse 2
He dances through the realms,
Unseen in the breeze,
Unleashing words of dissent,
In actions to appease,
No god nor mortal can resist,
The charm of Loki's guile,
For in the face of his deceit,
They fall like foddered rank and file.

As disorder reigns and empires fall,
His laughter does ring true,
Through the halls of Asgard,
Where fear and dread accrue,
Yet in his vengeance, lies a truth,
A lesson to be learned,
By the gods who scorned and shunned him,
Their hypocrisy discerned.

Verse 3
For Loki, Culture-bringer,
Shall play his final hand,
With Ragnarök around the bend,
The end of all that stands,
As Surtr's flames consume the worlds,
And gods in battle fall,
Loki's hand shall hold the ashes,
Of fate's unraveled sprawl.
And from the ashes of defeat,
A new world shall emerge,
With Loki's influence, renewed,
His essence shall converge,
In every act of violence,
Cunning, and deceit,
His spirit shall endure and thrive,
His vengeance not complete.

ALEISTER

Beneath the faded hues of Midgard's dawn,
A tale unfolds, of wisdom drawn,
From the gilded vaults of Jotun might,
Where shadows heed and Loki fights.

"From gold, forge steel," the trickster grinned,
From a rant forged in ire, to teach the wind,
A secret passed from scroll to ear,
A call to arms, to conquer fear.

With runes of old and secrets bound,
Occultist words did swiftly sound,
A call to transform the spoils of fate,
To weapons fierce, that fears abate.

"From gold, forge steel," a mantra sung,
By warriors bold, in every tongue,
Their riches spent on blades of war,
To face the storm and chaos' roar.

In the realm of Hel, where giants tread,
The trickster's message swiftly spread,
The golden hoard, a fleeting grace,
Reborn as strength, in this dark place.

The gleaming coins, now swords and shields,
With occult wisdom, their strength yields,
A metamorphosis of wealth and might,
To face the battles of day and night.

"From gold, forge steel," a lesson learned,
By those who faced adversity's turn,
Their fortitude, a testament clear,
To the magician's words, they held so dear.

In the heart of Midgard, as time wore on,
A Lokean's riddle, a siren's song,
A call to arms, for all to hear,
From gold, forge steel, and banish fear.

And thus, the madness of steel's birth,
From gilded chasms, to prove its worth,
A tale to tell throughout the years,
Crowley's gift, forged from gold and tears.

THE LOOM SINGS IN SILENCE

In the loom's soft murmur,
Where Norns weave with whispers,
The Web of Wyrd stretches—
An astral rune, a question in thread.

Strands intertwine, choice with fate,
Each knot a destiny, each gap a 'might be,'
As runes ink their sagas on the warp and weft,
Screaming in symbols, each line an incantation.

Black widow, you walk on trap divine!
Each bite an anarchy, each retreat a pause.
You pull at the strings, yet never sever,
In you, destruction finds its artful muse.

Loki, trickster at the loom's side,
Your colors blend with the Norns' somber hues.
Are you prisoner or poet in this grand design?
A god ensnared, yet ever the ensnarer.

Fimbulvetr looms like a storm in the north,
I find sanctuary in the Web's intricate net.
It asks without answers, secures without keys,
In its quandaries, I find my solace.

As prophecy pens the world's final lines,
This Web is my home, my fortress foundation.
I etch my runes, as the loom sings in silence,
Weaving my essence into tradition's seam.

Ah, the Web—forever a query, never an end,
An exercise at the edge of what's known and unfound.
It captures and frees, ensnares and eludes,
A wondrous terror, a terrifying wonder to stitch.

ODE TO ANGST

Disillusion swells,
Old scripts falling like dominoes,
Academia's charm has fled,
Mere parody of reality.
Yet, somewhere in the dim,
A seedling starts to grow,
Nurtured by self discontent,
It searches for its gravity.

O Angst, you restless wanderer,
What secrets do you hold?
A compass or a cage,
In you, which tale is told?
We sail upon your seas,
Though tempestuous and bold,
In ruckus and in quiet,
Our destiny unfolds.

Dilemmas, choices,
Chasms yawning wide—
Unveiling the abyss
Where our longings collide.
You're the spark and the darkness,
You are the blood's deepest hue,
You're the pressure of existence,
A mirror darkly viewed.

Oh, Angst! You're not a sickness
That a white coat could restrain,
You are the primal need,
Unearthing questions from the soil.
Each heartbeat's a revelation,
Your existence is our gain,
Teaching us the tightrope
Between the temporal and the eternal foil.

O Angst, you restless wanderer,
What secrets do you hold?
A compass or a cage,
In you, which tale is told?
We sail upon your seas,
Though tempestuous and bold,
In ruckus and in quiet,
Our destiny unfolds.

So, let's mingle with our dread,
Find rhythm in our fears,
Transform this trembling essence
Into passionate pursuits.
For within your stormy clutches,
We'll discover what endears,
Ignite a life of purpose,
Though subjective truth recruits.

Not a state to be vanquished,
But a portal to be passed,
Each anxious moment carries
The nerves of sacred rite.

O Angst, be my conductor
Through life's Ginnungagap vast,
Lead me to my Megin,
Where darkness turns to light.

Ah, Angst! You are no curse;
You're the dizziness of freedom,
An invitation, a provocation,
A challenging delight.
With you as my guide,
I'll traverse this open kingdom,
In your paradox, I find my resolve,
And I'm ready for the fight.

FINAL REVERIE

Intro

My warriors and I by the ship's side,
Calling upon Hel, ready for the tide,
Casting the runes, fire in our grip,
Lightning strikes down, with the Thunderer's rip,
A brother of mine, blood on his brow,
"If the Sisters cut early, are we ready now?"

Verse 1

Carve runes of war, on my shield and blade,
Plunge into battle, unafraid, unswayed,
Sing songs of conquest, with foes laid low,
Where the blood of Jotuns and dragons flow.
Feast in great halls, with a blade in my hand,
With Valkyries chanting, in Regin's grand land.
I'd contest to a clash, in Utgard's domain,
For a chance to fight gods, I'd embrace all the pain.

Musing

I'd don the guise of a mare, so sleek and so fair,
Lead stallions astray, with nary a care,
Spread secrets of gods, in the ears of the wise,
Transform to a fly, and flit through the skies.
I'd challenge Heimdall, in a game of disguise,
Steal Idunn's apples, right before her eyes,
Ride with the giants, through Niflheim's frost,
With lessons from Loki, no path is said lost.

Chorus

Hear the war drums beat? Echoes of the fray.
Feel the ground beneath? Shaking in dismay.
Steel yourself, heathen, as shadows cast anew,
When Ragnarök descends, just what will you do?

Wonders

Would you alter your form, like water to ice?
Or play with the gods, throw the Álfr-staves twice?
Would you heist what dwarves horde in caverns so
deep?
Or weave tales with the witch, as mortals do sleep?

Verse 2

I'd track down Odin, with laughter and jest,
Find out the secrets, from within his breast,
Ride with the wolf pack, through Ironwood's storm,
With Angrboda's touch, where the legends are born.
Challenge the powers, defy every norm,
Walk the fires of Muspel, watch Midgard transform.
With but a single turning, in warrior's rite,
I'd unleash all my fury, with unmatched might.

Chorus

Hear the war drums beat? Echoes of the fray.
Feel the ground beneath? Shaking in dismay.
Steel yourself, heathen, as shadows cast anew,
When Ragnarök descends, just what will you do?

THEATER OF THE ABSURD

In the Theater of the Absurd,
Where gods and mortals array,
Loki takes the stage,
Life's tragicomic display.
Neither hero nor phantom,
A paradox in a single breath,
Performing on the edge of the abyss,
Flirting with life and death.

Listen to Ginnung's overture,
A haunting symphony that weaves—
A tale of shifting forms,
An opera of endless eves.
Loki, you're the dramaturg
In the manuscript of fate,
The fourth wall
In a play both intricate and irate.

Masks upon masks, you don—
Serpent, mare, and flame—
Yet beneath, who are you
But an actor without a name?
The melancholy of your performance
Seeps through time's curtained sight,

A transient lament,
From stage left and right.

Feel the resonance in the boundless expanse,
A monologue so vast,
The tale of a protagonist,
Both first in line and last miscast.
But in the miscasting lies the brilliance,
In the error lies the art,
For you, Loki, are the mirror
A prop reflecting each transient heart.

Ragnarök's script written,
A climax penned in the book of years,
Yet you improvise, unfazed,
In a drama that transcends cheers and tears.
Troupe's choreography in your plot,
A tempestuous give and take,
You're the twilight zone of possibility,
Where realities break and make.

So, let this reading be your tribute,
An ode to your transient dance,
To Loki, it's an aside,
Peering across the theater's expanse.
You're the cue without a take,
The script without The End—
A complex apron of 'what-ifs,'
Life's most perplexing friend.

In your ceaseless role-changing,
An existential soliloquy unfolds:

The beauty and sorrow
Of a backdrop that never holds.
Oh, Loki, in your Theater,
In your parade's subtext so grand,
You remind us that life itself is
A playwright's tale, not always planned.

THE SONG OF GINNUNGAGAP

Intro
Loud, the chasm of Ginnungagap,
Where silence reigned supreme,
A seed was sown in deep cosmos,
Birthed from an ancient dream.
Oh, hear the song of creation,
The word of the primordial theme,
The hymn of all that ever was,
In the waves of Time's stream.

Verse 1
From a whisper, grew a wave,
An awesome melody,
Wandering through the Gap alone,
Piercing the silence, the decree,
Birthed from the need of Yggdrasil, before the giant
tree,
Through the vast expanse of Ginnungagap,
It flowed, forever free.

Chorus
Hear the song of Ginnungagap,
The hymn of world's inception,
The fabric of creation's heart,
The seed of Yggdrasil's conception.

In the silent vacuum, the note resounds,
The pulse of life's projection,
Heathen truths, our lore profound,
Guide us in reflection.

Verse 2
This pulse of power, the seed's refrain,
Gave rise to stars alight,
Galaxies spun in cosmic waltz,
In the twilight of the night.
From this single, sacred song,
Sprang forth the realms of light,
Ginnungagap's symphony,
The universe's birthright.

Chorus
Hear the song of Ginnungagap,
The hymn of Time's creation,
The echo of the Allfather's voice,
The pulse of the universe's foundation.
In the silent vacuum, the note resounds,
The birth of every nation,
Heathen truths, our lore profound,
Guide us in contemplation.

Verse 3
In this realm of echoes,
Where time and space begin,
The power of the word endures,
Its melody within.

The song of Ginnungagap prevails,
Beyond the cosmic din,
The universe's ballad,
Initial galdr, everything.

Chorus
Hear the song of Ginnungagap,
The anthem of existence,
The echo of Eternity's heart,
The symphony of persistence.
In the silent vacuum, the note resounds,
The melody of coexistence,
Heathen truths, our lore profound,
Guide us in resistance.

Outro
In silence and in sound,
In strife and in peace,
The song of Ginnungagap,
Its echoes never cease.
Through Heathen insights,
Our wisdom and release,
We hear the universe,
The song, life's masterpiece.

FRAGMENT

Born of naught—
Ice and flame,
I become.

Jotnar birthed—
My flesh, their home,
I dream.

Three loom near—
Fate's shears poised,
I sense.

Blades bite—
Universe quakes,
I fall.

Bones mountain—
Blood sea,
I fragment.

Skull sky—
Starry gaze,
I watch.

Weavers weave—
Destiny sealed,
I endure.

Rites ripple—
In Urd's deep,
I whisper.

Dispersed yet whole—
My essence sings,
I am.

Ravens circle—
Omens cast,
I foretell.

Endless cycle—
Doom's dark hymn,
I await.

ASH & ELM

Through Hvergelmir's seething depths,
Where primordial giants wept,
Three mighty gods did chance upon,
Two logs of ash and elm, foregone.

Odin, Hoenir, and Loki keen,
In the heart of Ymir's vast ravine,
Saw not just timber, coarse and crude,
But a nascent canvas, life imbued.

With divine intent and magic seidr,
They wove their power, nature's breeder,
In ash and elm, their essence cast,
A spell of life, forever vast.

Odin breathed into their forms,
Life's breath amidst the frenzied storms,
Hoenir gave them wit and will,
The mind's fire, never still.

But Loki, sly with witch's song,
In their veins let flow the throng,
Of his fiery, fierce essence,
Lifeblood's warmth, existence's presence.

Thus from deadwood, humans grew,
Under Ygg, arms wide and true,

Born of magic, divine decree,
In their being, the gods' flow free.

In humble wood, life was found,
On Midgard's solid, sacred ground,
By Odin, Hoenir, and Loki's grace,
Man and woman found their place.

Just two logs on a barren strand,
Became the genesis of man.
Remember well this ancient rite,
Of gods who made us, in the night.

GOLDEN NECTAR

Amongst a canopy of runes,
Where the roots of life entwine,
Lie secrets sealed in golden mead,
A hallowed, ancient wine.

From the sacred blood of Kvisar,
In Odin's mighty reign,
The Gods crafted liquid gold,
Through loss and honeyed pain.

A draught of wisdom, power, might,
Distilled in lofty halls,
A potent brew of knowledge,
That fate's hand must befall.

With each sip of eternity,
The gods their strength would find,
In the sweetness of the nectar,
Immortality defined.

But not just gods shall taste this spirit,
Or savor its potent charm,
For mortal men may seek it too,
Beware of lasting harm.

Still, seeker of the golden mead,
And the apples' treasured lore,
Drink deep of wisdom's sweetest draught,
And live hangover poor.

BIFRÖST

Three kindred spirits plotted their phase,
Under the canopy's exultant gaze.

Byleistr, the steadfast, with eminence bright,
Helblindi, mysterious, venerated the night.

With Loki's capricious mind at the helm,
They wove their magic, the realms to overwhelm.

From Asgard to rustic earth they'd span,
A ponderous design, a grandiose plan.

The bridge, in august raiment, did alight,
Beguiling all with its manifest sight.

Its pliant colors, a reflection so true,
Of the trio's essence, their steadfast hue.

Heimdall, the viceroy, with epithet clear,
Guarded the bridge, his mission sincere.

Yet under his aegis, tensions would grow,
The brothers' respite, now a tale of woe.

The implacable march of time did thresh,
Leading to Ragnarök, where fates would mesh.

The bridge, once boon, became battleground,
Where redoubtable kin their destinies found.

In the aftermath's hush, legends would deify,
The trio's ambition, reaching the sky

Their ponderous task, to realms it would bind,
A testament to vision, of heart and of mind.

FORGE OF THE HEATHEN

In forge where metal meets the flame,
We toil in Volundr's name.

Each strike of hammer, sweat that falls,
Prepares the anvil for our calls.

Our flesh, not slag, but grit does form,
Through trials, we are furnace born.

In homage to the Regin's kin,
We honor gods; their strength's within.

Our minds, the crucible refined,
Through mysteries, bind-runes align.

With Loki's wit, with Odin's sight,
We strike the paths by mani's light.

Where courage meets the blade's keen end,
As warriors, our honor we defend.

Each clash of steel, each battle cry,
Bellows of gods we magnify.

Our souls, the furnace of our oath,
In blood and vow, our promise clothed.

Each spark singes tales of old,
Wisdom's flame stokes fates foretold.

In sacred forge, pressure and might,
We shape our essence for the fight.

Offspring of gods, in veins their lore,
Heirs to realms where heathens soar.

RAGNARÖKRSÓNGUR

Ice bites—
Sky screams—
Jotuns rise—
Shatter dreams.

Mani bleeds—
Sunna dies—
Darkness reigns—
End belies.

Loki's vengeance—
Shackles burst—
Worlds end—
Curses first.

Thrym roars—
Skrym fights—
Golden gates—
End of nights.

Wolf's fangs—
Snake's hiss—
Angrboda—
Chaos' kiss.

Love's snare—
Hearts rend—
Gerd calls—
Freyr's end.

Surt's rage—
Flames scorch—
Giants march—
Nine-fold torch.

Snow's tomb—
Utgard's doom—
Jotuns stand—
Seal fate's loom.

Mímir's tears—
Wisdom's cost—
Future bleak—
All is lost.

Hear us now—
Gods beware—
Nail-ship sails—
End is here!

INFERNO

Verse 1
In Muspelheim I bide my time,
Like the bound count their days.
Ragnarök, the end's sublime,
I'm the maelstrom's scorching lay.

Pre-Chorus
Odin, hoarding wisdom's gold,
Freyr, trading steel for love.
Both of you aren't enough old,
To recall what I'm the bearer of.

Chorus
I am Surtr, hear my roar,
The end and the beginning.
When I'm through, you'll be no more,
And new tales we'll be spinning.

Verse 2
Loki, you're my trickster twin,
We laugh when gods are crying.
But jokes, get rid, be here to win,
We're the answer to their lying.

Pre-Chorus
Norns, you cut the threads of fate,
Like you're tailors trimming sky.
But even you can't estimate,
How all things live and die.

Chorus
I am Surtr, hear my blaze,
The final and the commencement.
In my flames, behold the gaze,
Of death and new refreshment.

Bridge
Heimdallr's horn, it sounds the call,
To Vígríðr, we march, sail and sing.
Illusions fall, and so will all,
But from the ash, what will we bring?

Outro
Understand, I'm not just flame,
I'm the maker in the void.
When I'm done, you'll know my name,
New worlds form to get destroyed.

Chorus
I am Surtr, hear my tale,
I'm destruction and creation.
In my story, all else pales,
To the inferno of salvation.

13 HAIKU

Odin's whispered kin,
Two ravens, but one fox—
Loki wears a grin.

Shadows grip the mind,
Hard truth slips through silent gaps,
New doors yet to find.

A mistletoe dart,
Balder's bane and mother's tears—
Loki plays his part.

Shape-shifter's disguise,
From mare to mother, flea, flame—
Loki's watchful gaze.

Ragnarök looms near,
Gods and Jotuns take their sides—
Loki laughs, no fear.

Garmr's howl foretells,
Guardian of icy gates,
Hel's hounds vast and fierce.

Fire warms the hearth,
Yet it also burns the hand—
Loki's double path.

Sigyn's love endures,
Bound by loyalty and pain,
For Ragnarök's dawn.

Rokkr offspring rise,
In chaos, ruin unfolds,
Old world turns to dust.

Untamed she remains,
In ice and shadow, she thrives—
Fate's womb, unshackled.

Jotnar stand immense,
Foe's fierce sculptors they become—
Storm and ice converge.

Confronting the depths,
Questions stir the ancient Well—
Wisdom's face changes.

Loki's fate unwinds,
Old gods fall, and new ones rise,
Cycle starts anew.

WHISPERINGS OF THE TRICKSTER

There I stood, amidst the shadows of the mighty halls of Asgard, watching as the Aesir reveled in their "victories", feasting and singing about the glory of their assumed lasting peace. How naive they were, and how my laughter resounded through the corridors, for they knew not what they had truly wrought. Yet, my thoughts, cunning and clever, held a truth they could not fathom – the truth that peace, as they understood it, was nothing more than a comforting lie.

Oh, how they clutched to their fleeting illusion like a babe to its mother's breast, believing that they had conquered all that threatened their realm. Yet, the very nature of existence itself is rooted in chaos, and that which seems stable is but a momentary respite from the storm. The Aesir's folly was in believing that they could tame the forces that had birthed them, not realizing that chaos is as much a part of their essence as it is mine.

Even now, as they celebrated their fleeting victory, the seeds of the world's undoing were already sown, and they were blind to the doom that awaited them. For they failed to comprehend that peace, as a constant state, was unnatural – a stagnating pool that would only breed decay. It is through struggle, through the clashing of opposing forces that one is truly alive, forging their spirit in the crucible of conflict.

And so, my thoughts found solace in this truth, for I was born of the raging storm, and I reveled in the dance of chaos that was existence. I saw the folly of the Aesir and the stale peace they so desperately sought, and I knew that it was my duty to open their eyes to the reality that they were too blind to see.

Where they sought to build a fortress of order, I would sow the seeds of discord. Where they sought to establish unshakeable bonds, I would remind them of the impermanence of even the strongest ties. In this, I would be the instrument of chaos, the harbinger of change, the Trickster who would bring balance to a world that had lost its way.

For it is not in the stagnant calm of a glassy sea that one finds their true potential, but in the raging torrents of a tempest that they are tested and tempered. To believe otherwise is to deny the very nature of reality, and in doing so, one would only hasten their own undoing.

And so, as the Aesir raised their goblets to toast their illusory peace, I smiled slyly, knowing that the cycle of chaos and order was eternal, and that their reprieve was but a fleeting moment in an ever-changing tapestry. For I, Loki, the embodiment of the dancing storm, would see to it that their eyes were opened to the truth, even as they sought to deny it.

Scan for more info
Or go to www.CultOfLoki.org

HAIL LOKI